fist of wind

                    womb
              womb not wound
        womb not wound   womb not
    womb not wound womb not wound
      womb not wound   womb not
                    und   wom
            womb   but   not
     womb   womb not wound   und
  b not wo   womb not wound   not wo
              womb not   not
                    womb not
    womb not wound   omb not
       womb   not wound   womb not
    womb not   womb not   not wound
         womb   mb not   omb not
            womb   wow not
              mb not   not wound
                     not wound   womb not
                   womb not   not
                      womb
                    not wound
                     womb

                        m
                 womb not wound
                    mb not wound
                  womb not
                 womb not wound
                    womb not

fist of wind
nefertiti asanti

Foglifter Press
2021

Book and Cover Design: Jason Lipeles and Miah Jeffra
Cover Image by Christa Pratt
Courtesy of Théo Mode
Copyright @ Nefertiti Asanti 2021
ISBN: 978-1-7369045-2-7

All rights reserved.

Cataloging-in-publication data is available from the Library of Congress

This book has been made possible, in part, by a grant from the Whiting Foundation

Printed in The United States of America

Foglifter Press
San Francisco, California
www.foglifterpress.com

table of contents

1
[day 27] every month

2
fist of wind

3
sometimes the seeds are tainted

4
split

6
exhume, or "exposure to american culture..."

10
things i wish to do on the rag

11
say my name

12
i have always had my hands

13
the present is an adolescent wit 3 wishes

15
among the living

16
womb not wound

17
Ritual for Black Survival

[day 27] every month

i desire

a red womb

that forgives

fist of wind

        then the tide came ripplin in makin soft the raw mouth of her
lifeline borderline flatline threatin to disappear her laughline bustline
waistline cuz ain't no breadline headlines full of redacted redlines
racin down her sixth wrist bangled in driftwood dangled
like a sunday palm draggin cross her chalk-lined shoreline

she kissed the lines on her hand & drew new lines in the sand
to mark what gotta be buried for a moment then washed away
too far away from her knuckles of grace & ambergris her
shoulders built in the belly of a shipwreck summoned &
discernin her bosom fillin the gullet of a teethin moon

        light slice right thru an eyeful of sky & leave
static on the island's sunken chest she grieves
unlockin the cage of her ribs to heave too many jellied
pupils near-black & cracked open in all directions
makin raw the soft mouth crumblin crumblin
under the weather's weight she throws her fist in the wind throws her fingers
open to grab the fabric of friction that
almost makes her   body   her   people a myth

sometimes the seeds are tainted

"Now new research is revealing that African-American women appear to be less susceptible to PMDD as well as to premenstrual symptoms overall—even though women who experience sex- and race-based discrimination are more likely to have PMDD."

> -From pr.web "Scientific Study Reveals Black Women Are Less Likely To Develop PMDD, The Most Severe Form Of PMS, And Have Less Premenstrual Symptoms Overall"

my body conceals weapons
a study cannot reach: sometimes
the weapons are seeds: sometimes
the seeds are tainted before birth:
tainted plot: tainted dirt: conquered
& cursed: sometimes the tiny seeds
are rosy rings: burning as they pass
through each fold: unfold into theyself:
pulling & pooling a dull dark syrup:
announcing the sludge of puberty
:or not pregnant: sometimes: seeds
break open to release 450 haints who
hold me ~~hostage~~ for a lifetime: work
can wait: i am more than worth
my weight in what i produce: healer
told me: *pain is information* &
my grandma & my great-aunt
& my mama & grandcestors already
paid the price: already passed the seeds:
i release in the year 2 thousand & nothing:
there is nothing i need to do to prove a study
wrong as two left shoes: wrong as a bent spoon
inside the flesh of a young mother giving birth
to modern gynecology: wrong as modern
gynecology: my body conceals wisdom
western medicine cannot teach: sometimes
the wisdom is seeds: planted before birth

split

i am learning to sit with my legs
crossed not ignoring the warmth
between my two thighs rubbing
against
the wishes of my clit
as long as i can be split
as long as i can hum while
i am split
i am asking for an invasion
to swarm against my personhood
orange & supple
so orange
it is golden
so golden
on another orb
it is cheap
abundant & abused: here
searching for a break in the skin

there is a rumor
there is a rumor

white whispers with no one
to tell it like it
is
the gospel truth
as long as i can
be spilt
hum while i am
spilt
i am as guilty

as the milky gum
of inkblot eyes
the smell of wet
exploding in the gash
of a blackened crater
mouth unending
the smell of tide
expanding to the gasp
of a moonlit scab
night does not fall
morning does not rise
& i cannot be whole
& live & die & live
to tell it
like it
Is

exhume, or "exposure to american culture…"

"Ethnic minorities in America will achieve majority by 2042, and due to their younger age distribution, will represent the largest proportion of women at risk for Premenstrual Dysphoric Disorder (PMDD)."

>-From the abstract of "Exposure to American culture is associated with Pre menstrual Dysphoric Disorder among ethnic minority women" by Corey E. Pilver, Ph.D., Stanislav Kasl, Ph.D., Rani Desai, Ph.D., and Becca R. Levy, Ph.D.

```
                              august in zen's room        came
                                          too late & i could not afford      to
                               exist   anywhere
    a forgotten patch of brooklyn                  inside me
         hope         unconscious              limbs         curl
                 crumple like a used napkin
save                                    my teeth my desire
     the            crawl      the       spider
                             human       picked me
        my building     my skin
                    before
                                              my mouth & their mouths
                           bile                          riding
                        with me
                                                easy
                                    body       be new
gone                            extracted
                              my hom e
                        between
```

i kept thinking about the time in august in zen's room the pain came & put me in an ambulance i could not afford because it was too late & i could not afford a cab to a 24 hour pharmacy that i didn't think existed anywhere near the projects at the edge of a forgotten patch of brooklyn. all things poured out from inside me from every orifice & i only hoped to be unconscious to sleep so my limbs would not curl & muscles would not tighten, crumple like a used napkin to say agony when there's no one that could save me. when the emt came, i explained thru my teeth my desire to sit & stand & lay across the ceiling or crawl along the wall like a spider that is confrontational with its deathdealer that so often is human. these humans picked me from breukelen projects not my building but my skin could tell another story & their training told them to believe my situation before anything that came out of my mouth & their mouths were poised with the familiar set of bile swishing about at the notion of riding down two flights of pissy project elevator with me. who was me anyway? & what was it worth that i had a body housing pain i couldn't afford? i should be easy compliant because the setting told them that this pain in my body should not be new to me, surely i've gone thru childbirth at least once, or extracted a bullet from my own gsw or stitched my own knifed skin surely pain is my homie & these strangers ain't got no business in the middle of a disagreement between old friends.

  domestic

                                                                     (~~not~~ violent)

not private

                communal   spilt in homes

                            [huh] blood is

          spilt in streets

libation   petition

                       creation

                                                      spectacle

       conjure myth

                                                 black spectre

           shoot to kill
           shoot until
           they be still

                              not alarm
                              not siren
                              not engine

                              no reason
                              for protest
                              ignited

                 just silent
                 volcano
                 erupted

                    slow lava
                        red smothers
                            huh! loud mouth
                    huh! fast-tail
        huh! bitch face
huh! bad weave
            huh! hoodrat
                    huh! fat back
                            huh! teen mom
                huh! chick dick
            huh! welfare
                huh! magic

                            prejudice
                            bathes in our
                            open wound

        ignorance
        refuses
        denies our

        [black]   childhood
                    neighbor 'hood
                        personhood

                            dignity
                            even in
                            living death

things i wish to do on the rag

[i] run a way my limbs are not used to running like my cradle is on fire but all i feel is heart & all that burns is sweat & i am so fast i am steam rising from my brown 'bows, my brown calves, my brown toes. i become bull, sea/red & charge belly low grazing ground rumble earth & i

[ii] laugh til head rolls clean off neck open revealing a swallow of stolen sunlight in the warmth of a joke i tell about lesbians & finger-paint but it don't sound nothing like the way my mama told it to me

[iii] dye black grrl magic myself a way out this flesh staining fabrics & declarations of independence & doves & chewing gum & wooden chairs & humans & hush puppies & mirrors & teacups. i especially wish to stain teacups, chipped & marked fragile when they are not really

[iv] fuck a way my mama fears i fuck on most anyone who will let me without consequence. fuck consequence. i am a piston.

[v] open in a way an unclenched fist does not exist: pulp palm

[vi] pulse in a way that welcomes worship whether or not i am on my knees

say my name

for the unnamed & the dead-named & the forenamed & the named present & the named thereafter

as i stare you down
the keyhole of my eyes

call SHOT/GUN

johnson's baby powder
drowns out the smell

of safe sulfur with every
intention of anointing oil

dabbed behind pierced
ears & formerly purled

necks rolling in & out
of the performance of hair

& hips: see me as skyline

on days you call night & i
never leave the ground

i have always had my hands

even when there was no field, no heads, no feathered things
to tend. had hands that knew *tender* swelled in front of the throat
when neck give reach   sunnin itself,   drinkin
up the light. dancin hands take a fistful of skirt & lift & lift & liiiiift
high-steppin over newly planted tomatoes, corn or like if i squat
over an unfamiliar plot i'll push   out   a funny-lookin seed & will
a thing to grow & grow whether or not i take myself past
the mason-dixon without that seed.   i still got hands

grateful to hold open a door for a pretty sateen thing passin thru
my eyes smile at the ground hopin a mistake will grow into a future
where my hand rests on the small of that passin thru pretty thing's back
& her lips touch the lip of the wine glass my lip touched & the clean
of the glass shine in competition with the shine of my teeth. half moon
in my mouth ain't too shy to present its tell-tale self here: we do not shake
hands like wrestin hangin fruit from the good neighbor's tree.

when these hands slow strangled the long neck of a used bass, the sound
come out never came out   again   the music changed mostly changed me,
gave me round breasts anybody could mistake for clementines, gave me
lips too full to fit on my face   only   so it found another & another,
gave me eyes too squintin-narrow to never not seem suspicious of kids
sittin too-too quiet in the back of the class or a man scuffed everywhere
but his shoes ~~or a river warmer than the air above it~~. the music changed
[my] hands, made it so my fist could fit into a swallow's mouth clench,
unclench without breakin the beak.

the present is an adolescent wit 3 wishes

i'm rubbin & rubbin & rubbin my tummy
like it's a magic lamp like a swole blue
genie finna uncurl in a smoke trail clear
out my vagina & lay 3 wishes on me   i'd wish
for a new tummy less swollen wit not-babies
not flat neither   i could set it down on my side
table   soft & doughy like the memory
foam pillow at my back proppin me up so i can
swallow oatmeal still warm in my mouth
maybe a 2nd wish would be a 2nd mouth
on the quickest side of my cheek smilin when i am not
smilin spittin like a real monster would spit
on doctors that don't know what the freak they doin

i most love me when i'm dippin my fingers
in the paint i make each month   vermillion
when i say it   feel like
i got caterpillars crawlin between my teeth
swear they buildin cocoons   i am careful
not to chew & swallow them too
pills water oatmeal tongue eddy in my mouth
my 2nd mouth recites picture book poems
in the silence between procedures
i ain't bled in such a long time i miss it

when my butterfly baby comes out
her cocoon i make my 3rd wish that bb
taps her little feet on my nose   kiss
my 2nd mouth then flutter away
to a good mommy who voice make dandelions
dance in a land where you don't need wishes
i say *vermillion* my blood would come

like silk   doobie wrap me in a sailor moon cocoon
so no one not even god could touch me

among the living

from the womb they mama gave 'em :: they release every egg :: they ever had inside :: them :: to a generous genderless gawd :: made in they image :: they gives birth to they self :: give name to they self :: gather they self up :: in the hands of everyone :: who ever loved them :: or wanted to love them & ain't really know how :: they love them some them :: they stops the blood :: sop it up with prayer :: or extraordinary guilt :: they belongs to they self & give nothing away :: they humor the gawd they pull :: out of they flesh :: pull away tissue & doubt :: pull fear away from muscle :: rename it heart :: pull hard edges away :: from splintered funny bone :: they smile :: this is the joke :: they walks the world on two hands :: pressed firmly :: on shoulders that mock cement :: they palms still soft from petting feral fur :: they fall down the tiniest tube & grow wings :: they flyy :: they black body flyy :: they land on alter earths :: byte down on other orbits :: they chew the bottom of the sky :: spit shooting stars from brown orbs :: they speaks of home knowing :: it could land in they lap & cut away the fabric :: or the tongue :: they decides :: they tailor & make everything fit loose :: they breathe voluntary & hunger deep

womb not wound

[concrete poem: the phrase "womb not wound" and its fragments are arranged to form the shape of a figure/womb]

Ritual for Black Survival

Become the pain Be the pain   Breathe the pain   Break open across pelvic
                                                                    thresholds
    Spelled out in your   mama's mama's maiden name   Rename your mama's
                                                                mama and
                                                            speak to her
                        The way the wind curdles in your womb
            Every body has a womb: a womb is the calabash of your soul
And it is dark, so dark it holds light   Hold your hand to the light until
                                                    Your fingers flame on
And your thumb is a torch song   to your sweat Remember to sweat milk
                                                            From every pore
that is not your bosom   Remember your core   Skin yourself red and alive
Like the first apple that told Eve that Adam aint shit
                                        Lilith is just outside the edge of Eden
                        Grow your own garden
Spread the wings on your legs   Become lush in your loins   Become tender and
                                                                        pink
    In the space between your lower lip and collarbone

Smoke your neck in lavender   Spill some other kind of blood from the you   You
could not let live outside the body   Do not keep your grief, I repeat
                                                Do not
                                                    keep your grief, I
                                                            repeat
    Do not keep your grief in a bag of your own skin   Love every sin
                                    you dared to commit
                                    In a name you cannot pronounce

Acknowledgements

Here's a list of acknowledgments for previously published poems:

Emerge: 2018 Lambda Fellows Anthology (Lambda Literary): "fist of wind"
Apiary Magazine: "split," "Ritual for Black Survival"
Hashtag Queer Vol. 2 LGBTQ+ Creative Anthology (Qommunicate Publishing): "things i wish to do on the rag"
Under the Belly of the Beast (Dissonance Press): "among the living"

"among the living" also borrows formatting from Evie Shockley's "my life as china"

Writing additional acknowledgments of the people that helped steward these poems has been the hardest part of writing this book.

In the time that I penned these words, so many of my connections to people I've love/d who love/d me have fractured, transitioned, erupted, dissolved, mutated, reverbed & re/birthed--so I say with certainty, much gratitude to my community: Linda, Mommy, Akeel, Salem, Ydedios, Drina, Aisha, Samantha, GJ, Ryka, Xandria, Vanessa, Nava, Tim, Marrion, Tyrell, Starr, Alan, Joe, MJ, Alex, Mama Lisa, Lisa, Lapree, Erica, Kirwyn, Kalima, Sophia, Zen, Itiola, Meghan, Mona, Danielle, Saniya-Sincere-Destiny, Rozz, Katrina, Kaydee, Arisa.

Additional thanks to the Watering Hole, EmergeNYC (2015), Anaphora Arts, Lambda Literary, Foglifter, Radar Productions, Winter Tangerine, Still Here SF, Hurston/Wright Foundation, Stellium Literary Magazine, & Queer Cultural Center.

fist of wind is dedicated to my Great Grandma on mama's side, Grandma Patsi, & Aunt Karen.

Nefertiti Asanti is a poet born and raised in the Bronx and a recipient of fellowships and residencies from the Watering Hole, EmergeNYC, Lambda Literary, Anaphora Arts, Winter Tangerine, and the Hurston/Wright Foundation. Nefertiti is also a 2021 PEN America Emerging Voices fellow. Currently, Nefertiti serves as prose poetry editor of *Stellium Literary Magazine*.

About the cover artist

Christa Pratt is a visual artist based in Brooklyn, NY. Born in the Bronx with roots in South Carolina, they studied Fine Arts Painting at Pratt Institute in Brooklyn, NY. They were an Artist-in-Residence for the Museum of Arts & Design's Artist Studios Program in 2017, and their work has been featured in exhibitions at Arts East NY and Spring/Break Art Show NY.

Rooted in the San Francisco Bay Area, Foglifter Press is a platform for LGBTQ+ writers that supports and uplifts powerful, intersectional, and transgressive queer and trans writing through publication and public readings to build and enrich our communities as well as the greater literary arts.

Eye the margins.

www.foglifterpress.com

www.ingramcontent.com/pod-product-compliance
Lightning Source LLC
Chambersburg PA
CBHW072210100526
44589CB00015B/2464